WAKE UP!

NOBODY MATTERS

BLACK LIVES, WHITE LIVES, YELLOW LIVES, RED LIVES, BROWN LIVES, REPUBLICANS, DEMOCRATS, POLITICIANS, RICH, POOR, YOUNG, OLD, GOVERNMENT OFFICIALS, GAY PEOPLE, STRAIGHT PEOPLE, COMMUNISTS, ANARCHISTS, ACTIVISTS, SOCIALISTS, ATHEISTS, SECRET SOCIETIES, LUCIFERIANS, DEEP STATE, ONE WORLD ORDER OLIGARCHS, CONSERVATIVE, LIBERAL, BABIES, HUMAN LIFE

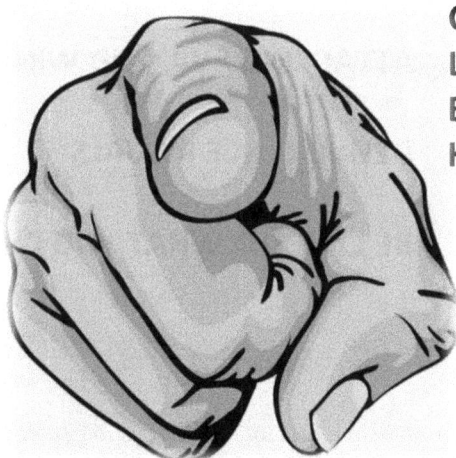

DON'T MATTER

By Fr. Francis Pompei ofm

TABLE OF CONTENTS

CHAPTER 1	WORDS THAT DIVIDE	7
CHAPTER 2	SATAN OR GOD	19
CHAPTER 3	GOD'S LAWS: YOUR REPORT CARD	26
CHAPTER 4	ORIGINS OF EVIL	31
CHAPTER 5	HOW EVIL WORKS	39
CHAPTER 6	HOW DEMONS AND SPIRITS CAN ENTER YOU	52
CHAPTER 7	ATTACKING EVIL AND WINNING	60
CHAPTER 8	DELIVERANCE RITUALS	70
CHAPTER 9	BE CAREFUL WHAT YOU CHOOSE	81
APPENDIX		88
BIBLIOGRAPHY		90

COPYRIGHT
All rights reserved

No part of this publication may be reproduced, stored in a retrieval system or transmitted in any form or by any means, mechanical, electronic, photocopying, recording or otherwise without the prior written permission of the publisher.

EDITOR: Trish Pompei

INTRODUCTION

My guess is that the title of this book is offensive to both individuals and groups. My response to you is that the **TRUTH** can be offensive and threaten those who have been **deceived** and **obsessed** by **EVIL**, Negative Thoughts, Half Truths, and Lies.

This should offend and tick you off even more and trigger your anger that wants to challenge, confront, punish or cancel me.

Congratulations, if you do, then you prove that **YOU** matter, **I DON'T**, and need to be silenced and eliminated.

One of the things that matter are **WORDS.** Words convey thoughts that ignite emotions and feelings that, in turn, drive our actions. All negative, hostile, and violent actions begin with the thoughts and images that words put in our minds.

When we choose to think about and dwell on them, they invite more thoughts and images that inflame our anger like a volcano ready to erupt. Whoever and whatever is threatening us, our desires, values, agenda, narrative, or life, needs to be silenced by whatever means.

Because Words matter, then the definition and meaning of Words are at the root of the hostile and divided world we live in today. Words are interpreted by individual people and interpreted different, and here in lies the problem. Everyone assumes that their understanding of words should be and is the same as everybody else's. **NOT SO.**

The gasoline that has been poured on the fire of Words is there are too many damn words. Words, Words, Words, Words, News 24/7, media platforms, texting, email, chat lines, opinion shows, Google, Face Book, Internet, Websites, I pads, I phones, I tablets, I watches, Twitter, I quit and unholy sh-t.

Everybody wants to be heard, but nobody wants to 'Listen' and know real people, only their words which they don't really care about if they don't fit their position and narrative.

If you don't believe this then watch all the news networks in one day. Same ol' crap, panels, debates, experts, sources and officials that always end with screaming words louder and louder at each other, and then the anchor cuts them off, thank God, with "We've run out of time and need to take a break for a commercial".

They all end up fighting, name calling, and labeling one another. This is supposed to be the news that is helping people to form their conscience, share possible answers and real solutions. Journalism and the news media have become biased propaganda and hate.

The truth is that the news in America is really entertainment. I think the News has mimicked the Jerry Springer show for years. The only thing lacking is they haven't taken their clothes off and started pulling hair and fighting.

So, if Words matter, then the definition and meaning of Words is crucial to a common understanding of what we're talking about in order to not just find common ground, but real answers to real problems. Even more important to just solving problems is establishing a personal respectful relationship with one another that goes beyond any disagreement.

EXAMPLE: When someone asks me if I am a racist,
I say **'No', I'm Fran Pompei**, who are you?

With most of our communication today via technological devices, human beings have lost the personal connection with one another, which is one of the reasons why **nobody else matters.** Persons and people are simply **words** in texts, phone conversations, computer emails, twitters and messages. Technology has raped us of our mystery and put us in boxes, categorizing and judging us with no interest in knowing us.

For years now the fascination with technology has given humanity many good things, but inherent with it is horrific evil and destruction, an evil that is demonic, divisive, and extremely ADDICTIVE. If you don't believe this, just try to take a cell phone away from a teenager.

So much for listening to and being with family, friends, strangers, and seeing their faces and reading their real feelings for more than a half minute twitter or 2 minute text. They **DON'T MATTER!**

Because all the above is unfortunately extremely addictive, without many knowing it, they are **psychologically obsessed** and can't stop it or have no desire to, because it gives them Power, Control, and Pleasure.

Anyone who points this out or challenges them is the enemy trying to take the drug away and must be eliminated and cancelled. Welcome to the new world of **'AWOKE'**, the latest catch **WORD** that means, **"Who the heck knows what it means"**?

One thing for sure, like many other groups or movement's Words or slogans, there's those who agree and those who do not. Those who do not,

DON'T MATTER.

CHAPTER 1

WORDS THAT DIVIDE, SPARK ANGER, RETALIATION, AND VIOLENCE, DRIVEN BY SELF-RIGHTEOUSNESS.

YOU ARE A

- RACIST
- HOMOPHOBE
- MISOGYNIST
- SEXIST
- NAZI
- WHITE SUPREMACIST
- DICTATOR
- AWOKE
- LIAR
- FAKE
- EVIL
- ANTI-AMERICAN
- RICH ELITIST
- SWAMP MONSTER
- HYPOCRITE
- BIGOT
- FEAR MONGER
- BIASED
- CRIMINAL
- TROLL

These are the Words of **'Identity Politics'** which focuses on a person you want to hurt or cancel. These are the **Words** of **NOBODY MATTERS**!

WHAT THE HECK DOES THE WORD 'MATTER' MEAN ANYWAY?

MATTERS: Human beings deserve respect, protection, absolute right to live and be, regardless of skin color, race, gender, and ethnicity.

RESPECT: A feeling of deep admiration for someone or something elicited by their abilities, or achievements- Due regard for the feelings, rights, or traditions of others.

RIGHT: Morally good, justified, or acceptable. Those principles and behaviors that benefit not just the person, but others, and the common good as found in objective natural law

THOSE WHO THINK THEY MATTER CAN DO 'NO WRONG'

- "It's my life, I can do what I want"
- "Who made you God?"
- "Who the heck are you to tell me what is right?"
- "I'm free to choose whatever I think is right, so get out of my face."
- "If it feels Right, do it"
- "If it feels Good, do it."
- "Forget about Right or Wrong!"
- "If you get caught, lie."

These are the words of those who feel their actions and decisions are being challenged, threatened and held accountable.

They represent what's called **'Subjective Morality'** which has become the dominant morality these past 60 years.

SUBJECTIVE MORALITY:
- Morals are all **HUMAN-MADE BY INDIVIDUALS, GOVERNMENTS**, and **GROUPS** and can vary from person to person with no accountability or responsibility.

OBJECTIVE MORALITY:
- There are **many universal laws that make some morals objective and unchanging**, such as murder. Killing someone in cold blood, and not because of self-defense, is not morally justified. It ends a person's life, hurts their family, and makes you the monster.

- One who believes in God believes that **our morals come from God,** the creator of all reality and us, and **because God cannot change, this means that many of his laws are not subject to change and thus are objective.**

- People of faith point out the universal laws God has made, such as the **Ten Commandments**, the **Two Great Commandments of Jesus**, and The **Five Pillars of Islam**.

WHY WE NEED MORAL LAWS AND OBJECTIVE TRUTHS

Satan, fallen angels, demons, gods, and aliens have infected our physical bodies **DNA** and through telepathic knowledge transfer, opened our minds to know and experience **both good and evil**. With this came not only evil, but suffering, violence, and death.

HUMANS, ARE BOTH GOOD AND EVIL

GOOD	EVIL
LOVE	LUST
FORGIVENESS	PUNISH/ SELF-HATRED
COMPASSION	HATE
RESPECT	ABUSE
HOPE	DESPAIR
FREEDOM	FEAR
RECONCILIATION	VILLAINIZE
PEACE	VIOLENCE AND WAR
JUSTICE	BIAS/ PREJUDICE/ ELIMINATE
INNOCENT	ALLEGATION WITHOUT EVIDENCE
CREATE	DESTROY
TRUTH	NEGATIVE THOUGHTS/ HALF TRUTHS/ LYING
GENEROSITY	TAKING/ STEALING
SHARING	HOARDING
EMPOWERING	CONTROLLING

JOY	PLEASURE
COMMUNITY	ANARCHY/ SOCIALISM/ COMMUNISM/ MARXISM/ DICTATORSHIP
CONTENTMENT	ENVY/JEALOUSY
WHOLENESS	SUFFERING
EMBRACE	ABUSE
LIFE	DEATH/KILLING
SELFLESS	GREED
FAMILY	INDIVIDUALITY/ NARCISSIST
AFFIRM	CANCEL
GOD	YOU ARE GOD AND YOUR DESIRES

Because of Satan, Fallen Angels, Spiritual Beings who messed with our physical DNA through sex and experimentation, they created us as hybrids, mixing our DNA with theirs, which was unnatural and forbidden by GOD, our creator.

The result is what we call human nature is now capable of both Good and Evil and therefore is in need of laws, restrictions, boundaries and accountability. **Why, to keep us from destroying others and ourselves, which is and was the goal of Satan and Evil from the beginning.**

WAKE UP! BECAUSE OF EVIL, NOBODY MATTERS

BLACK LIVES DON'T MATTER

700 MURDERS AND 4,000 SHOOTINGS IN CHICAGO IN 2020-

- RWANDA GENOCIDE 596,400 BLACK PEOPLE RAPED AND MURDERED BY THEIR BLACK BROTHERS AND SISTERS.

BROWN LIVES DON'T MATTER

- ISIS/ TALIBAN/ TERRORISTS:
- OVER 1 MILLION IN THE IRAQ- SYRIA, AFGHAN WARS, BEHEADING AND KILLING THEIR OWN COUNTRYMEN AND WOMEN

YELLOW LIVES DON'T MATTER

KHUMER ROUGE, KILLING FIELDS

- 300,000 CHINESE
- 90,000 MUSLIMS
- 2,000,000 VIETNAMESE CAMBODIANS- KILLING THEIR OWN RACE

RED LIVES DON'T MATTER

- **WOUNDED KNEE MASACRE**: 300 WOMEN, CHILDREN, AND MEN
- **SAND CREEK MASSACRE**: 230 WOMEN, CHILDREN, MEN

WHITE LIVES DON'T MATTER

NAZI'S UNDER HITLER
- 6,000,000 JEWS KILLED (LIKELY MORE)
- 9,000 HOMOSEXUALS KILLED
- 200,000 MENTALLY ILL AND DISABLED KILLED

CHILDREN'S LIVES DON'T MATTER

RADICAL ISLAMIST LIKE 'BOKO HORAM' ENSLAVE YOUNG WOMEN AND SMALL GIRLS FOR SEX, THEN KILL THEM WHEN THEY ARE DONE.

HUMAN LIFE DON'T MATTER

- **ABORTION: A WOMAN'S LEGAL RIGHT TO COMMIT PREMEDITATED FIRST DEGREE MURDER OF AN UNBORN OR PARTIALLY BIRTH HUMAN BABY.**

- **50,000,000 (MILLION) MURDERED BABIES SINCE ABORTION WAS MADE LEGAL. TAKE A GOOD LOOK! MULTIPLY IT BY 50 MILLION.**

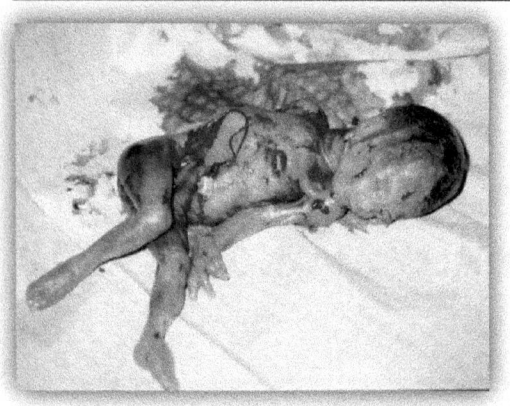 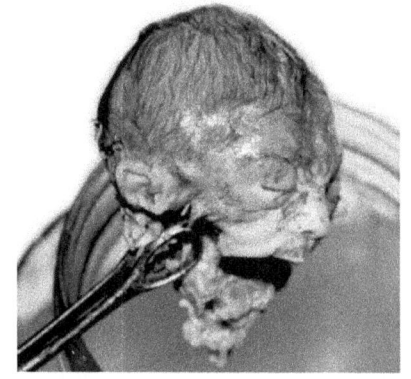

Center for Bio-Ethical Reform "Copyright abortionNO.org"

Pro Choice, Abortion Activists, and Planned Parenthood, YOU are living proof that black, white, brown, red, yellow lives and human life
DON'T MATTER!

YOU ARE IN DENIAL, AND ARE BEING SEDUCED BY EVIL, POWER, SEX, MONEY, AND HEDONISM.

"ALL LIVES MATTER IS BS"

It is not **'RACISM'** that is the driving force of violence, hatred, and killing, it is **SATAN AND EVIL** that is the source, but nobody wants to talk about Satan and Evil.

You either don't believe in them, are afraid of them, or you are **DISCIPLES** of them.

Human life does not matter since Satan and Evil Spirits taught **humankind there is great Power and Pleasure** in violence, and killing.

For your information, the names are Azezal/Semyaza
(Original fallen angels and their cohorts)

GOD'S INVITATION TO SAVE YOUR CONSCIOUSNESS, MIND, SOUL AND WILL

- **REPENT**: ADMIT THAT YOU HAVE SINNED AGAINST GOD AND HIS COMMANDMENTS.

- **REMORSE**: FEEL THE PAIN AND SUFFERING YOU HAVE CAUSED OTHERS.

- **CONFESS:** TO GOD AND THOSE YOU HAVE SINNED AGAINST.

- **EXPRESS RESPONSIBILITY** FOR WHAT YOU HAVE DONE.

- **COMMIT TO CHANGING YOUR ACTIONS**, BY DOING PENANCE TO RETRAIN YOUR MIND.

- **ASK TO BE FORGIVEN BY GOD AND** BY YOUR VICTIMS. APOLOGIZING AND SAYING YOU'RE SORRY ISN'T ENOUGH.

JUDGEMENT: Whether you go to heaven or hell for your actions is up to the God who created you and wants you to repent and choose life, because he unconditionally loves you and will forever.

EXAMPLE:

Those in power and individuals who pledge their political support that killing an unborn baby is a woman's legal right to commit premeditated first degree murder have sinned against God, the baby that wants to be born and live, and the sacredness *('Matters')* of human life.

THOSE WHO DISAGREE WITH THIS TRUTH HAVE BEEN SEDUCED BY SATAN AND EVIL INTO BELIEVING THEY ARE 'GOD' AND DETERMINE WHAT'S RIGHT AND WRONG. THEY ARE IN DENIAL AND INSTRUMENTS OF EVIL.

If anyone says, "I believe in God", but does not keep His commandments, **they are liars,** *and* **the truth is not in him.**
(1 John 2:12-3:23)

To all of you who are government leaders, politicians, activists, who claim you are devout Christians and believers that are personally against killing of unborn babies, but support, legislate Pro Choice policies, you are liars and in grievous Sin.

Your problem according to the Word of God is not with Pro Life or me, but with the God who created you, and you will be held accountable, if not in this life, in the next.

"Jesus said, **it would be better for him to have a millstone hung around his neck and to be thrown into the sea than to cause one of these little ones to stumble."** *(Lk. 17:2)*

Read the above again so you can be
REALLY 'AWOKE' SPIRITUALLY
and save yourself.

"My Father, the God who created and loves you, sent me, His son, into the world to share in your suffering and death that Satan and Evil corrupted you with.

Through my Resurrection I have opened a 'Portal' from this world to Heaven. Satan, Evil, Flesh and Blood cannot enter.

I will recreate your bodies to be **Perfect** to dwell in Heaven for ever. The Glory I will manifest in you, you can't even begin to imagine how great it will be."

CHAPTER 2

SATAN OR GOD

BLACK LIVES,
WHITE LIVES,
YELLOW LIVES,
GOVERNMENT
LEADERS,
DEMOCRATS,
POLITICIANS,
RICH, POOR,
BABIES,
YOUNG, OLD,
ACTIVISTS,
SOCIALISTS,
ATHEISTS,
DEEP STATE,
OLIGARCHS,
RED LIVES,
BROWN LIVES,
REPUBLICANS,
CONSERVATIVES,
LIBERALS,
STRAIGHT PEOPLE,
GAY PEOPLE,
COMMUNISTS,
ANARCHISTS,
SATANISTS,
SECRET SOCIETIES,
LUCIFERIANS,
ONE WORLD ORDER,
HUMAN LIFE,

NONE OF THE ABOVE MATTER!

IF YOU DON'T BELIEVE IN GOD AND HIS COMMANDMENTS, **YOU BECOME 'GOD'**, DETERMINING WHAT'S RIGHT; ACCOUNTABLE AND ANSWERING TO NO ONE, BECAUSE <u>NOTHING IS WRONG</u>.

WHAT JESUS SAID ABOUT SATAN AND EVIL

- "A Liar & The father of Lies"   Jn. 8:44
- "A murderer"   Jn. 8:44
- "The Tempter"   Mt. 4:3
- "The Prince of Demons"   Mt. 12:24
- "He perverts the Scripture"   Mt. 4:4
- "The god of this world"   2Cor. 4:4
- "The Deceiver of the World"   Rev. 12:9
- "The Seducer of Adam and Eve"   Gen. 3:1-20
- "He has a Kingdom"   Mt. 12:26
- "Evil men are his sons"   Mt. 13:38
- "Eternal fire is prepared for him"   Mt. 25
- "Seeks to devour believers"   1 Peter 5
- "The Enemy- The Evil One"   Mt. 13:39

CONCLUSION:

- **Do Satan and Evil really exist? The language of Jesus certainly indicates his own belief in the existence of Evil and Satan as a person.**

TWO PATHS FOR YOU TO CHOOSE-
Which one are you choosing? You can't have both.

PATH ONE

SATAN/ EVIL:
POWER-PLEASURE AND IMMORTALITY

- THIS DIMENSION OF THE UNIVERSE- PHYSICAL AND SENSORY IS THE **ONLY REALITY** FOR ALL ETERNITY.

- TO BE LIKE SATAN AND FALLEN ANGELS, CAST OUT OF HEAVEN, WHO CHOSE TO REPLACE GOD AND BECOME GODS. THEY OFFER HUMANS THEIR DIVINE KNOWLEDGE, TO BECOME LIKE THEM, GODS.

- THEIR MORALITY: *(Satan And Evil Have None)* ANYTHING GOES, NO ACCOUNTABILITY TO ANY ONE, LIFE IS HERE AND NOW AND THE GOAL IS TO GRAB ALL THE GUSTO YOU CAN; NO LAWS, NO GOD, NO COMMANDMENTS, ONLY YOU AND YOUR DESIRES.

POWER:
POLITICAL, ECONOMIC, PERSONAL, FOR PLEASURE, CONTROL, AND DOESN'T MATTER HOW YOU GET AND MAINTAIN IT. NOTHING IS WRONG AND YOU ARE ACCOUNTABLE TO NO ONE. THE END JUSTIFIES THE MEANS.

MONEY:
MONEY IS POWER AND ANY MEANS TO GET IT IS ACCEPTABLE BECAUSE YOU ARE GOD AND ACCOUNTABLE TO NO ONE. NOBODY MATTERS EXCEPT YOU AND OTHERS WHO THINK AND BELIEVE LIKE YOU.

SEX: UNBRIDLED, ORGIES, SADOMASOCHISTIC TORTURE, PEDOPHILIA, RAPE, SEXUAL SNUFFING OUT. IMMORTALITY WITH CONSTANT ERECTION AND ORGASMS IN THE NEW DNA CREATED BODY.

HEDONISM: THE EXPERIENCE OF EXTREME PLEASURE NO MATTER WHAT YOU DO OR HOW YOU DO IT:

- PLEASURE IN KILLING- BEHEADINGS, TORTURE, MURDER
- PLEASURE IN RITUAL SACRIFICES TO OTHER GODS
- PLEASURE IN HUMAN SACRIFICES TO SATAN AND OTHER DEMONS
- PLEASURE IN THE DRINKING OF BLOOD
- PLEASURE IN KILLING BABIES
- PLEASURE IN ORGIES
- PLEASURE IN DESECRATING GOD: BLACK MASSES BY DESECRATING THE RISEN CHRIST IN THE EUCHARIST USING A WOMAN'S VAGINA.

SATAN'S ULTIMATE PLEASURE IS EXPERIENCING INTIMACY WITH SATAN HIMSELF, WHO WAS THE GREATEST OF ALL GOD'S CREATIONS AND BEARER OF THE SUBSTANCE OF

GOD'S DIVINITY (I.E. 'LIGHT'), WHY ONE OF HIS NAMES WAS **LUCIFER** *(Light Bearer)*.

HIS EARTHLY AND PHYSICAL **PLEASURES REPLACE** THE HOLY SPIRIT, WHICH IS THE 'UNCONDITIONAL LOVE' OF GOD.

GOD- UNCONDITIONAL **LOVE**
SATAN- UNCONDITIONAL **PLEASURE**

IMMORTALITY:
SATAN AND EVIL WILL ENABLE SCIENCE AND TECHNOLOGY TO DISCOVER THE MYSTERIES OF OUR HUMAN DNA AND GIVE IMMORTALITY TO OUR PHYSICAL BODIES THROUGH CLONING AND GENETIC ENGINEERING, RECREATING OUR THOUGHTS, MEMORIES, AND CONSCIOUSNESS WITH ARTIFICIAL INTELLIGENCE.

WE WILL BE GIVEN THE DIVINE KNOWLEDGE OF SATAN, FALLEN ANGELS, AND DEMONS, TO TRAVEL THE UNIVERSE AND DIFFERENT DIMENSIONS, AS GODS, NEVER DYING.

IT IS A DECEPTION AND LIE.
WHEN CHRIST COMES, SATAN, ALL HIS MINIONS AND THOSE WHO HE SEDUCED AND FOLLOW HIM, WILL BE CAST INTO HELL FOREVER WITH NO ESCAPE.

'AWOKE' TO THIS FACT!
IF IT'S TRUE AND A REAL POSSIBILITY FOR YOU, ARE YOU WILLING TO TAKE THE RISK?
'AWAKE',

PATH TWO

GOD, THE FATHER, SON, AND HOLY SPIRIT
Unconditional Love and Eternal Life

GOD CREATED US BECAUSE HE LOVES US

- "Before I knit you in your mother's womb, I knew you and have always loved you.

- Satan brought evil into physical reality and humans through lust for sex with human women and knowledge to mix human DNA with theirs, which God had forbidden.

- Satan and his fallen angels, Nephilim *(demons, after their physical bodies died because they lost eternal life)* have the goal of enslaving us to worship them, and destroy those who don't with suffering and death.

- God sent Jesus to save us from this end when we sin, if we confess.

- Jesus conquered evil's greatest power on the cross and that is **fear** of suffering and death as the end of our life and existence.

- Jesus resurrection opens the divine portal to heaven by his recreated body, **no longer subjected to temptation, suffering, evil or death.**

- "I am the resurrection and the life. Anyone who believes in me, when your physical body dies, I will raise you up to live forever in heaven."

- "I will wipe away your tears. There will be no more suffering, death, or **EVIL.**"

- St Paul: "We can't even imagine the glory that God will manifest in our bodies."

- "I have come to give you life, and life to the fullest."

- "I have come to give you joy and make your joy complete."

"I condemn no one. Those who do these things condemn themselves.

CHAPTER 3

<u>GOD'S COMMANDMENTS</u>
YOUR REPORT CARD

If you are guilty of any of the following and **don't REPENT, CONFESS and CHANGE**, you may think you are not accountable to anyone and escape punishment**, <u>BE WARNED</u>, that eternal Death and Hell lasts a lot longer than your physical bodies and desires that Evil has seduced and addicted you too.**

EVERY ONE WHO IS READING THIS BOOK, READ CAREFULLY AND SLOWLY WHERE YOUR SOUL AND SPIRIT ARE AT WITH THE GOD WHO CREATED YOU.

1. <u>**YOU SHALL HAVE NO OTHER GODS BEFORE ME.**</u>
   When you become addicted and slaves to Money, Power *(Personal, Political, Psychological, and Religious),* Greed, Hedonism, Sex, the Occult, Satanism, Sports, Electronics, Possessions, Alcohol and Drugs, you have sinned **by replacing God and been seduced by Demons who will destroy you.**

THESE ARE SINS AGAINST GOD AND OTHERS, YOU WILL BE HELD ACCOUNTABLE!

2. YOU SHALL NOT TAKE THE NAME OF THE LORD IN VAIN.

Name Calling, Identity Politics, Labeling, Judging, Attacking, and putting all people regardless of Race, Gender, or Creed In the same category, is **wrong** and leads to Anger, Hatred and Violence.

THESE ARE SINS AGAINST GOD AND OTHERS, YOU WILL BE HELD ACCOUNTABLE!

3. KEEP HOLY THE SABBATH DAY.

Choosing to **Not** believe and having a personal relationship with God is a sin, **because YOU become god, accountable to no one for** violence, power, oppression and corruption. **You are in Sin, destroying yourself and others.**

THESE ARE SINS AGAINST GOD AND OTHERS, YOU WILL BE HELD ACCOUNTABLE!

4. YOU SHALL NOT KILL - MURDER.

- **Abortion**: Killing of babies in a mother's womb before and after birth **is Premeditated First Degree Murder. It Is First Degree Murder** for the doctor who commits the horrific killing and 2nd degree murder for those assisting. For those believing and supporting it as a woman's Right, it is **evil driven, wrong, and the most heinous sin against God and life.**

"It would be better if a millstone be put around their neck and thrown into the sea." (Mk 18:6)

- Premeditated killing of anyone by Terrorists, Violent Groups, or anyone, is **Wrong** and **a Serious Sin against God as 'Creator'.**

- Assaulting, except for Self-Defense, **is Wrong and a Sin against God and others.**

- Those who support, assist, and stand by and watch **are wrong and commit a Sin.**

THESE ARE <u>GRIEVOUS SINS</u> AGAINST GOD AND OTHERS, YOU WILL BE HELD ACCOUNTABLE!

5. <u>YOU SHALL NOT COMMIT ADULTERY.</u>
Rape, Pedophilia, Fornication, Adultery, Sex Abuse, Prostitution, Pornography, Sex Trafficking. **Those who do these things are sinning grievously against God and their victims.**

THESE ARE SINS AGAINST GOD AND OTHERS, YOU WILL BE HELD ACCOUNTABLE!

6. <u>YOU SHALL NOT STEAL OR COVET YOUR NEIGHBOR'S GOODS</u>

- Tearing down public or private statues without the owner's permission, or the legal process of the community, is wrong, illegal, **and a Sin.**

- Rioting, looting, robbery, embezzlement, taking of any ones property or goods **is wrong and a sin against others and God**.

- Intentionally destroying another's Reputation and Life is **Stealing.**

THESE ARE SINS AGAINST GOD AND OTHERS, YOU WILL BE HELD ACCOUNTABLE!

<u>YOUR JUDGEMENT DAY: INESCAPABLE</u>

- God Matters and His commandments are the answer for you, me, and humanity. His commandments are the foundation of our Declaration of Independence, Constitution, and Bill of Rights.

- When your physical body and senses die, your Consciousness, Mind, Spirit and Soul will be held accountable by the God who created you. You will be judged according to your **Deeds**.

- **HELL**: Eternal Damnation, Nothingness, No Love, No God, No Light, No Peace, Only Suffering, Torment, Isolation, Loneliness, and most of all No Hope, and No Coffee Breaks, if evil doers do not repent, ask God for forgiveness, and change. **You can deny this, but it is a fact and your future, if you do not repent.**

- **You will be held accountable for your deeds when your body dies, whether you believe it or not. It is the truth that you will not escape.**

- **ETERNAL DEATH** LASTS A LOT LONGER THAN EVIL PEOPLE'S POWER, PLEASURE & VIOLENCE. **CHOOSE 'LIFE'**

SATAN! "YOU DECEIVED ME, YOU BASTARD!

HELL DOES NOT NEED YOUR BELIEF IN IT TO EXIST. THAT IS A FACT. SO MUCH FOR YOUR POWER TO CONTROL REALITY!

CHAPTER 4

ORIGINS OF EVIL

What is important is that all reality in the Spirit World, as well as the physical, including you and me, shares in the **Unconditional Love** and **Light** that is God. By reflecting on God as Light, we can appreciate who and what we are to God and understand the magnitude of what Satan and the fallen angels lost and can never get back.

Put simply, in choosing to be 'God' and have his own kingdom, power, and servants (humanity), who Satan and his fallen angels would corrupt, control, and manipulate with knowledge of Good and Evil, lost their Light and the Unconditional Love of God.

As you read the following Scriptures, it will become clear that **God is Light,** and all Creation, you and me, share in His light. We are beings of Light, but because of what Evil has done to us, there is now darkness, Sin, Suffering and Death.

LIGHT AND DARKNESS: WE ARE LIGHT MADE PHYSICAL

- "**GOD IS LIGHT**, in him there is no darkness at all." Note we are not told that God is a light, but that **HE IS LIGHT**. Light is His essence, as is Unconditional Love. (1 Jn. 5)

- "Believe in the light while you have the light, so that you may become children of light." (Jn. 12:36)

- "This is the message we have heard from him and declare to you, God is light; in Him, there is no darkness at all." (1 Jn. 1:5)

- When Jesus spoke again to the people, He said, "I am the light of the world. Whoever follows me will never walk in darkness, but will have the light of life." (Jn. 8:12)

- "If we do not have the light, we do not know God. Those who know God, who walk with Him, are of the light and walk in the light. They are partakers of God's divine nature, having escaped the corruption in the world caused by **evil desires**." (2 Peter 1:4)

- "God is light, and so is His Son." Jesus said, I am the 'Light of the world'. You are all children of the light and children of the day. We do not belong to the night or to the darkness."(1 Thes. 5:5)

- "As adopted sons of God, we are to reflect His light into a world darkened by sin. **Our goal in witnessing to the unsaved is "to open their eyes and turn them from darkness to light and from the power of Satan to God."** (Acts 26:18)

To help clarify what all this means in the big picture for you and me, run this through your Mind. Every day it is the choice between **Physical Reality** *(The World and the Flesh as Jesus referred to it, subject to our human desires, Sin, Suffering, and Death)* and the Spirit, **God's light**. I cannot say it any better than God did, as stated before,

"I place before you "Life and Death." Choose Life!"
(Deut. 30)

SUMMARY:

- God did not create Evil. Conscious spiritual beings, created by God in Heaven were sent to guide and live among humanity—angels.
- They lusted after human women, seduced and had sex with them, which was forbidden by God both for humans and the fallen angels.
- These spiritual beings in physical bodies wanted to be "gods," having their own Kingdom and followers. Because they had knowledge greater than ours, they interfered with our DNA through sex and genetic engineering; cloning; cross breeding; producing evil monsters who taught knowledge to humans that God forbade.

"We were created a little less than the angels..."
(Hebrews 2:7)

Thus, **EVIL** came into the physical realm permanently and with it, Suffering and Death. If this sounds like a Science fiction movie and fantasy story *(Myth)*, it may not be anymore, because of recent archeological and scientific discoveries.

- We now can manipulate chromosomes and DNA.

- We now can mix different DNAs to create new species.

- We now are on the cutting edge of artificial intelligence. We now can clone a human body.

- We are developing telepathic mind control techniques and artificial intelligence

Maybe what the Theologians and Scripture scholars thought was a myth, little by little, may become actual recorded history.

CONCLUSION:

- Does the Devil and Evil really exist? The language of Jesus certainly indicates his own belief in the existence of a personal devil.

- Satan and Evil have affected, rather infected, all of physical reality, which includes our physical bodies— brain included.

- Evil can infest our MINDS with **thoughts** and **images** that awaken our emotions, feelings, desires, passions, and affect our choices, if we let it. Evil, ultimately intends to seduce, control, enslave, destroy us, and use us to destroy each other.

Take a moment to read the above three conclusions and remember them. Why? You cannot defeat the Enemy, unless you know who they are, and how they operate.

According to Jesus and the New Testament, Satan and Evil exist and are conscious beings with divine knowledge having powers. If you do not believe in this, remember your problem is not with me, but with Jesus.

- *"The one who does what is sinful is of the Devil, because the Devil has been sinning from the beginning. The reason the Son of God appeared was to destroy the Devil's work." (1 Jn. 3:8)*

- *"I am afraid that just as Eve was deceived by the serpent's cunning, your minds may somehow be led astray from your sincere and pure devotion to Christ." (2 Corinthians 11:3)*

- *"Submit yourselves then to God. Resist the Devil, and he will flee from you." (James 4:7)*

If all this Satan and Evil talk is starting to frighten you, relax, because there is not only good but Great News coming. By the time you finish this book, Satan and Evil will be frightened and terrified of **YOU**.

EVIL EXPOSED: HOW IT AFFECTS OUR MINDS

If the only thing Evil can do is put thoughts and images in your minds, then your Mind is the battlefield where you are in continual warfare with Evil that is trying to seduce, control your Will and decisions, and ultimately destroy you and all of us.

SCRIPTURE: REGARDING YOUR MIND

- *"Do not be conformed to this world but be transformed by the renewal of your mind, that by testing, you may discern what is the will of God, what is good and acceptable and perfect." (Romans 12:2)*

- *"We impart this in words not taught by human wisdom, but taught by the Spirit, interpreting spiritual truths to those who are spiritual. The natural person does not accept the things of the Spirit of God, for they are folly to him, and he is not able to understand them, because they are spiritually discerned.*

- The spiritual person judges all things but himself to be judged by no one. For who has understood the mind of the Lord so as to instruct him, but **we have the mind of Christ.**   (Corinthians 2:13-16)

- *"For God gave us a spirit not of fear, but of power, love, and self-control." (Timothy 1:7)*

Jesus is teaching us that, in fact, we are in school, and He is retraining our <u>Minds</u> to think and operate the way His does. This is not a once and for all deal, but takes a whole lifetime to learn and get better at it. The good news is the more we do it, the better we get, and the more natural it becomes.

The point here is that the Lord is telling you what to do and how to do it every day.

The more you replace the negative thoughts, images, half-truths, and lies that Evil and the world infest your mind with every day, the more you will feel the freedom from your fear and worrying.

"Finally brothers, whatever is true, whatever is honorable, whatever is just, whatever is pure, whatever is lovely, whatever is commendable, if there is any excellence, If there is anything worthy of praise, think about these things." (Phil. 4:8)

"Do not be Afraid or let your hearts be troubled. Trust in the Father and Trust in Me.

The power in YOU is truly greater than the evil powers, principalities, and demons that are in the world.

Learn to not only believe this, but to use the power of my name and attack evil whenever it is attacking and trying to seduce you.

I am and will be there to punish and cast it out together with you."

CHAPTER 5

HOW EVIL WORKS
Pay Close Attention!

"All of Creation Groans for the Salvation of the Christ"

Evil puts thoughts and images in your mind, tempting you to choose, download, and think about them. When you choose to think about them, that is when powers and spirits can almost immediately enter your feelings, emotions and desires, with fear, anxiety, lust, anger, etc.

When you continue to DWELL on them, they intensify your emotions and desires to act on them. This can lead to **obsession**, when you cannot stop your mind from thinking about and dwelling on your problems or suffering. This is like putting gasoline on the fire of your passions and desires.

Then you become like a volcano ready to erupt and the only way to release these desires and emotions is to act on them and do the Evil that promises you pleasure and satisfaction. When you succumb to this temptation and attack, you choose (Your Will) to do the Evil.

It's like a computer. I hope you are a little computer savvy. If you are, then you have probably seen the irritating blue screen with the message that your computer is infected with a virus. Doesn't it frustrate you? And it usually happens when you are right in the middle of something important.

Next is that little icon at the bottom of the screen that starts pulsating, and the following message pops up: "Your computer is infected with a Virus. Click here and download a free program that will clean your hard drive from the virus." Here is the question for you, should you click on the free anti- virus program that promises to restore your computer? If you are computer literate, your answer is **NO**. Why, because **it is the VIRUS**.

This is exactly how Evil works on your Mind. It promises you everything, but in the end destroys you and others. Evil has power over us while we are in these physical bodies, because they have not only interfered with our DNA physically, but also our Minds and infected them with the capacity to 'know' and experience Good and **Evil**.

This is one of the reasons Jesus came to save us, that is, to give us authority and power over Evil. The only problem is that many clergy and religious leaders never taught us about Jesus' power to deliver and how to do it. The good news here is that Jesus will teach you how, later in this book. Be patient, He will do this later and then do it with you. Now that is something to get excited about and look forward to!

St. Paul describes the battle that goes on in our minds and how Evil has power over us.

- I know that the law is spiritual; but I am unspiritual sold as a slave to sin. I do not understand what I do. For what I want to do I do not do, but what I hate I do. If I do what

I do not want to do, I agree that the law is good, as it is no longer I who do it, but it is sin living in me.

- For I know that good itself does not dwell in me, that is, in my sinful nature. I have the desire to do what is good, but cannot carry it out.

- For I do not do the good I want to do, but the Evil I do not want to do—this I keep on doing. Now if I do what I do not want to do, it is no longer I who do it, but it is sin living in me that does it.

- Therefore, I find this law at work, although I want to do Good, Evil is right there with me. For in my inner being I delight in God's law; but I see another law at work in me, waging war against the law of my mind and making me a prisoner of the law of sin at work within me.

- What a wretched man I am! Who will rescue me from this body, that is subject to death? **Praise to my Lord Jesus Christ, for in Him there is no condemnation.** (Rom. 8:1)

Let us take this and apply how Evil works on our minds, with an issue of the day. The following is an article I wrote and submitted to a local newspaper.

EXAMPLE: IDENTITY POLITICS

My greatest fear is that Identity Politics has led us to divisions, not only in our political views, but in our churches, communities, and what's worse: in our families and with our friends. From division, Identity Politics has led to anger and then to violent anger that wants to retaliate and punish. The more we engage in it, the more we become obsessed by it, demonize people, and are filled with hatred. The final choice is open harassment, violence, and then civil war.

I believe the power and forces that are driving this are not just part of our human nature, but demonic. Evil is the one word that is mentioned often, but never discussed, understood, or addressed how it seduces, influences, and then controls people's minds, will, and actions. Maybe it is time to not only discuss answers and solutions to the issues, but also the evil forces that are the real enemy influencing, obsessing and possessing terrorists, rapists, murderers, traffickers, gangs, and even ourselves.

In the Christian Scripture it says, "Our struggle is not against flesh and blood, but against the rulers, principalities and powers of this dark world and the spiritual forces of Evil in the heavenly realms." (Eph. 6:12)

The reason Evil seems to be triumphing is that most people do not believe in Satan or Evil powers. Not a bad tactic on Satan's part to keep people powerless by their choice to not believe, while He's busy achieving his ends without any resistance

Politicians, media, news networks and their 'so called' professional panels, debates and 'reliable' sources have produced NO answers or solutions, only division **AND**

HAVE GIVEN BIRTH TO THEIR EVIL CHILD, <u>IDENTITY POLITICS.</u>

Identity Politics is merely the "politically correct" term for hate and demonizing those who disagree with us. The hidden and inherent evil in identity politics is the **Self- Righteous Justification** Evil uses to, little by little, control our minds with negative thoughts, half- truths and lies that overwhelm and drive us to verbal and physical violence.

Evil is the real enemy, but for the most part no one wants to talk about it and those that do are considered out of touch with reality. Yet, Satan and Evil, or whatever you call them have existed and been experienced from the beginning of humanity and recorded in every major and ancient Religion.

Evil does not need our belief in it to exist. It does exist and my guess is that most of us have heard, seen, or experienced something that seemed so surreal that our minds were unable to comprehend it. And we recoiled in terror because it was beyond human. Because we do not acknowledge its existence, we give it free reign to influence our minds, will, and actions.

Personally, I am tired of politics, media, news networks, panels, experts, Republicans and Democrats. I'm tired of narratives, and most of all I'm tired of words, words, and more words that Identity Politics offers—words that fuel demonizing people, hatred, and violence.

Humanity needs to expose the real enemy, **Evil,** and

what it has done and is doing to people and humanity. My prayer is that this will be a **"wake up"** call for all of us tempted and seduced by Identity Politics.

This is how Evil, by our choosing to download, think about, and dwell on the thoughts and images it puts in our minds, progresses to a point where we are driven to act on them—ultimately destroying ourselves and others.

I categorize these Evil thoughts into:

- **NEGATIVE THOUGHTS:** Doctor: "I'm sorry, but your tests came back positive."

- **HALF-TRUTHS:** "You are terminal and going to die."

- **LIES:** "Death is the end of your existence and life."

CASTING OUT' EVIL THOUGHTS FROM YOUR MIND

Using the analogy of **NOT** clicking on and downloading the free program to delete the virus in your computer; **don't download** the evil thoughts or images.

HOW DO YOU DO THAT?

HERE ARE THE STEPS OF WHAT TO DO:

1. Say **NO** the minute you become aware that you are afraid or being tempted and seduced. Use your **WILL,** choose to say **NO.**

2. Then Say, **'LORD'**, the same as you did the minute you experienced a problem or suffering when you were four years old and cried out for Mommy. This step is not magic, but the most difficult of all, and the essential element to getting your degree in Trust. You are using your **WILL** to say **'NO'** and choosing to focus off the negative thoughts, half-truths and lies and on Jesus right there with you.

3. Evil is not going to give up attacking and tempting you, especially when it has successfully trained your mind for years to download everything into your mind and immediately think about and dwell on them. In this step, you will need to say **NO** many times, and probably for the rest of your earthly life, because this is the way the Lord will retrain your Mind.

EXAMPLE:

The doctor tells you that the results of your tests are positive for cancer. This is a serious negative thought, right? If you choose to download and think about it, immediately a flood of more half-truths and lies enter like, "Its terminal, I know it. I'm going to die. It's the end of my life; what about my family." Then the images of suffering download and "How am I going to deal with this? I can't do it." Does this sound familiar? And the worst is yet to come—Fear.

The more you choose to think and dwell on those incoming thoughts and images the more intense they get. Your emotions and feelings kick in almost instantly, and **Fear** turns into Terror as you see there is no way out. Your mind keeps racing and racing out of control.

It is at this point that people of faith pray and ask God to help them to make the problem go away, be healed and put to rest. If they keep praying and praying, and the cancer or problem does not go away, gets worse, and death is imminent—the next lie of Evil is

"You're wasting your time praying and going to church. If God really loved you like He said, He would heal you."

This is **'the moment of truth'** for you and your relationship with Jesus. Are you going to Trust Him no matter what, or are you going to succumb to the Fear and Evil's lies that are tempting you to doubt.

If you choose to doubt and stop trusting in the Lord, Evil will lead you into the dark hole of despair with only your problem and without hope. This is, as I said before, the goal of Evil—to destroy you and keep you from the power of the Lord and the Truth.

Focusing on God, who is with you, is an act of Trust, which is what we are here in school to learn and grow in.

Keep reading, because there is more good news to come. Replace the negative thoughts, half-truths, and lies with the TRUTH."

EXERCISE: Take your time when reading the Truths to replace those **evil thoughts** that are at the root of much of your suffering. Memorize them, burn the **Truth** in your mind and use the truth to counteract the evil thoughts.

FEAR/ANGER/DOUBT/DESPAIR

LIES-HALF-TRUTHS- NEGATIVE THOUGHTS:

- Death is the End.
- The tests will be positive— I know it. I'll never endure this.
- Why is God punishing me?
- What's the use of praying? God isn't doing anything.

TRUTH: Jesus, what do you say?

- "Don't be afraid or let your hearts be troubled. Trust in God and trust in me." (Jn. 14:27)
- "I am with you every day until the end of time." (Mt. 28:20) "Where there is fear, love has not been

perfected, love dispels fear." (1 Jn. 4:18)

- "While you are in the world you will suffer (*and your bodies will die*), but don't be afraid, for I overcame my fear of Suffering and Death and will be with you in yours." (Jn. 16:33)

GUILT/SELF-HATRED

LIES-HALF-TRUTHS- NEGATIVE THOUGHTS:

- I hurt others deeply. I am selfish and destroyed someone and myself.

- I can never get back what I lost. God could never forgive me. I am embarrassed, ashamed, and just want to hide. I'm going to hell. This feeling of guilt will never go away, no matter what I do. I don't like myself for what I did. I don't think I can live with this every day, for the rest of my life.

TRUTH:
- To the woman caught in adultery, Jesus said: "Does anyone condemn you? Then neither do I condemn you. Go and sin no more." (Jn. 8)

- What I do, I do not understand, for I do not do what I want, but what I hate. For I do not do the good I want, but I do the Evil I do not want. Because I am a slave to sin, what a wretched man I am! Who will deliver me from this mortal body? "Praise be my

Lord Jesus Christ **for those who are in Him, there is NO condemnation!**" (Romans 8)

- The Prodigal Father never asked his son who returned home what he did or what his sins were. He said, "Put rings on his fingers, give him a cloak, kill the fatted calf, and let's celebrate." (Lk. 15)

- The Lord unconditionally loves you before you sin, while you are sinning, and after. His love for you never changes. Look at a Crucifix and you'll see it.

SUFFERING

LIES-HALF-TRUTHS- NEGATIVE THOUGHTS:

- I will never be able to go through it.

- It will always hurt this badly and get even worse. Where is God, and why me?

- I won't be able to do the things I use to. What's the use of living?

- It is so frustrating. Will it ever stop?

- I don't understand why we have to suffer for so long. Life is hell.

TRUTH:

- "Therefore, we are not discouraged; rather, although our outer self (physical body) is wasting away, our inner self is being renewed day by day." (2 Cor. 4:16)

- "For this momentary suffering is producing for us an eternal glory beyond all comparison, as we look not to what is seen but to what is unseen; for what is seen is transitory, but what is unseen is eternal." (2 Cor. 4:18)

- "The sufferings of the present are as nothing, compared to the Glory that will be revealed in us." (Rom. 8:18-23)

- "While you are in the World you will suffer, but don't be afraid, for I overcame the world....and I am with you every day, until the end of time." (Jn. 16:13)

- "If we share and experience the sufferings of Christ, we will share in His resurrection." (Rom. 8:17)

DEATH

LIES- HALF-TRUTHS- NEGATIVE THOUGHTS:

- I am dying. It is the end of my life, dead, forgotten, wake, funeral, and buried.

- I will never see my loved ones or experience joy

and happiness again.

- I can't stop thinking about it, and I'm afraid of the suffering ahead and my life ending.

- This is it. I'm never getting out of this one. What is going to happen to my family and loved ones? I am so frightened and feel so alone and abandoned by God.

TRUTH:
- "Our Citizenship and Home is in Heaven, and from it we also await a Savior, the Lord Jesus Christ." (Phil. 3:20)

- "I am the Resurrection and the Life. Anyone who believes in me will never die, and anyone who dies believing in me will live forever." (Jn. 11:25)

- "We can't even begin to imagine how great will be the Glory that the Lord will manifest in us." (Rom. 8:18)

- "For if we have been united with him in a death like his, we will certainly be united with him in His resurrection." (Rom. 6:5)

- "Do not let your hearts be troubled. Have faith in God; have faith in me. In my Father's house, there are many dwelling places. I will come back again and take you to myself, so that where I am, you also may be." (Jn. 14:1)

CHAPTER 6

HOW DEMONS AND SPIRITS CAN ENTER YOU

It is of the utmost importance that you read slowly, reflect on, and do a survey of your life to understand how you may have willingly or **unwillingly** allowed Evil Spirits, Powers, and Demons into your mind, body, and seduce your Will.

This is serious territory and many churches have neglected to talk about the Occult, Evil rituals, and practices that may seem innocent and entertaining, instead open the floodgate to Demons, Spirits and Principalities to enter our minds, attach to us, and torment us with the goal of eventually controlling and using us for their demonic intentions.

GOD'S WARNING AND CONDEMNATION

- **"Let no one be found among you who sacrifices his son or daughter in the fire, who practices divination or sorcery, interprets omens, engages in witchcraft, or casts spells, or who is a Medium or who consults the dead.** Anyone who does these things is detestable to the Lord, and because of these detestable practices the Lord your God will drive out those nations before you." (Deut. 18)

- "Many of those who believed came and openly confessed their evil deeds. A number who had practiced **sorcery** brought their scrolls together and burned them publicly. In this way the word of the Lord spread widely and grew in power." (Acts 19:18-20)

- "Do not turn to Mediums or seek out Spiritualists, for you will be defiled by them. I am the LORD your God." (Leviticus 19:31)

- "I will set my face against the person who turns to Mediums and Spiritualists to prostitute himself by following them, and I will cut him off from his people." (Leviticus 20:6)

- "When men tell you to consult Mediums and Spiritualists, who whisper and mutter, should not a people inquire of their God? Why consult the dead on behalf of the living?" (Isaiah 8:19)

ASTROLOGY

- "And when you look up to the sky and see the sun, the moon and the star, all the heavenly array, do not be enticed into bowing down to them and worshiping things the LORD your God has apportioned to all the nations under heaven." (Deuteronomy 4:19)

- "Do not practice divination or sorcery." (Leviticus 19:26)

- "The idols speak deceit, Diviners see visions that lie; they tell dreams that are false, they give comfort in vain. Therefore the people wander like sheep oppressed for lack of a shepherd." (Zechariah 10:2)

FALSE GODS AND IDOLS

- "You shall not make for yourself an idol in the form of anything in heaven above or on the earth beneath or in the waters below. You shall not bow down to them or worship them; for I, the LORD your God, am a jealous God, punishing the children for the sin of the fathers to the third and fourth generation of those who hate me." (Exodus 20:4-5)

SEANCES

<u>Seances</u> are occult Evil rituals and practices conducted by Mediums whose power is to contact the dead or persons who have crossed over to another level of reality. A séance means to "sit" with spirits from another world.

Sometimes Mediums hear otherworldly voices along with seeing spirits manifesting themselves from another world. These Demons and Spirits can speak through the Medium or with the use of Ouija board or writing on an object.

TRUST ME, it's not your 'Uncle Tanoose' whose voice you're hearing, but a Demon or Spirit that is mimicking your Uncle.

DIVINATION

Divination is the attempt to gain foresight and knowledge about the <u>future</u> through various methods. These are your fortune-tellers, Leaf or Palm readers, and Psychics who may use Crystal Balls and Tarot cards all for the sake of predicting events and telling your future. Once again you are opening yourself, mind, soul, and Will to the Spirit World other than the Holy Spirit and the Lord. Say **NO** to this crap and to anybody who is or wants to get involved in it. Ouija boards and Tarot cards make good kindling for a fire. **Get to it!**

SATANISM

Satanic cults have been officially documented in Europe and North America as far back as the 17th century.

The Satanic Church was established in America in the 1960s. These Cults/Churches are worldwide. The strange and violent practices, like black masses where a Catholic Consecrated Host (Eucharist-Body and Blood of Jesus) is stolen and desecrated with a woman's vagina.

In addition they are involved in bazaar orgies with children and adults and horrific sexual rituals and actions, murder, Human Sacrifice to Satan, including suicide. They appeal to the lowest and darkest parts of our fallen nature. Believe me when I say they are more prevalent than you think.

Remember Satan and Evil hates humanity, yet they want to **STEAL OUR LIGHT** which they lost and we still have because of Jesus. They ultimately want to make us their slaves and disciples by seducing us with the pleasure they give through unbridled sex, power, money, hedonism, hatred, torture, and destroying others and God's creation.

EXAMPLE:

In the 1990s in the United States, there was the 'Vampire Cult', led by Rod Ferrell, who murdered a family in Florida using a horrific sadistic Sacrifice Ritual. Ferrell was only 16 years old at the time of the <u>murders</u>.

The news reported that this cult took drugs, performed blood and sex rituals and orgies, and later killed Naomi Ruth Queen and Richard Wendorf. Though rare, human sacrifice has definitely found its way into today's society, often as a Ritual to please Satan and experience other worldly pleasure when doing it. (Example Terrorists: Rape of children and beheadings)

Sounds like a science fiction movie, doesn't it, but tragically it is not. This is the battle between Good and Evil that the Lord gives us His power to confront. So, **DON'T BE AFRAID, REMEMBER WE WIN THE WAR**, and my hope is that this Manual will give you the Trust in the Lord and the Tools to win the battles, not just for yourself, but for others who are Evil's victims.

SPELLS

Spells are technically recitals, <u>words spoken by a Wizard</u> or one who has chosen and been given the power by evil to affect persons, places or things. Tokens, charms, combination of various plants and animal parts for a brew, to putting pins in a likeness of the person that the spell is cast on. The true power of the spell is in the recitation of certain ancient chants,

'Hocus Pocus" Crap

For ages, people have been using spells to unleash misfortune upon others, some for general bad luck and others for revenge and even something that will cause the death of their victims. Spells can be made to even affect sleep with demonic nightmares.

DEMONISM

Probably we have all seen movies where the Evil Bad Guy or Woman invoke the Gods and Specific Demons to give them power to conduct their actions, especially to torture, murder, or destroy.

Demonism seeks to summon the power of specific <u>Demons</u> to empower the petitioner to carry out their evil deeds. Since ancient times, occultists have believed that they can harness the power of these dark Spirits and Demons. Those who teach and practice Demonism use ritualistic incantations to summon different demons for various purposes in many cultures throughout history believed to be responsible for humanity's most violent acts. <u>Serial-killers</u> and brutal dictators have been thought to be under the control of these demonic influences, perhaps even causing most of humanity's atrocities.

<u>ADD TO THIS:</u>

- Certain Demonic Computer Games And Movies
- Witches Covens
- New Age Rituals
- Voodoo
- Santeria
- Drug Cults

Your reaction to all this may be one of doubt that this is really happening or write it off as psychological disorders and just a bunch of crazy people.

My response to you, as a Priest involved in the Deliverance Ministry is,

> **"They are real, exist, and these groups, people, and practices are RAMPANT, but operate in the background *(Secret societies)* lest they be discovered and destroyed."**

Because they are real and exist was and is my reason and motivation for writing this book so you **WON'T** be frightened of anything you have read so far, but instead, experience and use the power God in Jesus has given us to **ATTACK, PUNISH, BIND and CAST them OUT.**

CHAPTER 7

ATTACKING EVIL AND WINNING

Are you scared yet with all this talk about Satan and Evil? Is your Fear thermometer rising with thoughts that there just may be more than the Evil humanity and we generate?

According to what God said about Satan, Evil has and continues to corrupt humanity and all physical reality with the intention to tempt, experiment with, enslave, steal our Light, soul, consciousness, and ultimately destroy us.

I offer as proof that this is real by the Fear that enters your mind when you consider and think about Satan and Evil.

Why? **FEAR** is Evil's greatest power.

I found the following article that will put some flesh and blood reality on what Satan and Evil are up to, according to the Word of God and what Jesus said about them.

Pay close attention to the following story that demonstrates that Evil not only **TEMPTS** us to wrongdoing, but **SEDUCES** us with Good things and activities that we eventually **ADDICT** to.

This is the way Evil slowly influences our Will to **REPLACE GOD**, Church, and our Church family with our desires for **things** and **activities** that we want to do that give us pleasure, entertain us, power, and make us feel good.

KEEP THEM BUSY by Ralph Andrus

Satan called a worldwide convention of demons. In his opening address to his evil angels, he said, "We can't keep Christians from going to church. We cannot keep them from reading their Bibles and knowing the truth. We can't even keep them from holding onto their conservative values, but we can do something else. We can keep them from forming an intimate lasting relationship and experience with Christ. If they gain that connection with Jesus, our power over them is broken.

So, this is what I want you to do. I want you to distract them from experiencing Jesus Christ and having a personal relationship with Him, throughout their day. Let them go to church, let them have their conservative lifestyles, but steal their time so they cannot gain that experience and relationship with Jesus.

The Evil angels asked him, "How shall we do this?

- Keep them busy with the nonessentials of life to occupy their minds with more things to buy and more things to do. They'll not only be distracted, but addict to them, like sports, shopping, electronics, TV, and cell phones. This is how their addiction will replace God, their Church family and even ignore their friends and loved ones, too busy starring at their cell phones and tablets.

- Tempt them to spend, spend, then charge, charge, and charge it. Convince husbands and wives to work long hours and overtime so they can afford their lifestyles. This will keep them from spending time with their families and talking to Jesus.

- See to it that every store and restaurant in the world plays suggestive and seductive music, trashing Christian values. This will jam their minds and break their relationship with Jesus.

- Fill their coffee tables with magazines and newspapers. Pound their minds with the news 24 hours a day.

- Invade their driving moments with billboards. Flood their mailboxes with junk mail, sweepstakes, mail order catalogs and every kind of newsletter and promotion offering free products, services and false hopes.

- Even in their recreation, let them be excessive with working out, hunting, fishing, yoga, sports and more sports. Have them return from their recreation exhausted, stressed, and less time for faith and family.

- When they go to church, involve them in gossip and small talk, and make them bored so their minds wander off to all the things and activities they have become addicted to. They'll keep checking their watches, wishing the service to hurry up and be over. That way they won't experience Jesus while they are there. **INTERESTING, ISN'T IT?**

Like I said before, Evil wants us to doubt and deny its existence, because by doing so, it renders us powerless over it and gives it free reign to complete its agenda.

Somehow I believe we all know it is real because of our inability to wrap our minds around genocide, mass murders, rape, child abuse, torture, beheading which even the media labels "demonic."

This core belief and response to Evil is in us, because despite being influenced and infected by it, we are still beings of **Light**, connected to God, which enables us to recognize both **Good** and **Evil**—in this case, Evil.

The Word of God describes these beings, entities or powers as the real Enemy.

- *"Our battle is not against flesh and blood, but against Powers, Principalities, and Rulers from the Kingdom of Darkness." (Eph. 6:12)*

- *"When you pray, say, Our Father who art in Heaven...**Deliver Us from Evil.**" (Mt.6:13)*

- *"These are the signs that will follow all those who believe, whomever they lay their hands on will be healed... In my name, they will cast out demons and spirits." (Mk. 16:17)*

STOP:

The above words of God in Jesus are critical for all who read this book and for all of humanity. Read them again one more time before proceeding.

The reason they are critical is Jesus overcame Satan's temptations of power and greed when He was tempted in the desert. When He was condemned, scourged and crucified, He overcame the temptation of doubt, despair, fear of Suffering and Death. He did so by **choosing to focus on His Father**, moment by moment instead of the temptation and suffering. Then He **chose from moment to moment with His WILL, to Trust His Father**.

Just as Jesus conquered Evil through the power of His Will and Trust while in a flesh and blood body like ours He has paved the way and shown us what to do, how to attack, defeat, and deliver ourselves and others from Evil.

- *The power that is in us now is greater than the powers that are in the world. (Eph. 1:19)*

Do you believe this? More importantly have you experienced the Lord's power that is greater than the evil you face?

I thought at this time it would be helpful to clarify the difference between **Deliverance and Possession**, which I have found very confusing to people when talking about or experiencing evil spirits and powers.

I found the following psychological descriptions of conditions and accompanying manifestations. In addition to defining them, they also offer answers and therapeutic guidelines in dealing with the people who are experiencing these phenomena. Being in the deliverance ministry, I have found them to be very helpful in developing an appropriate spiritual and psychological approach when ministering with a person for their deliverance.

OPPRESSION – OBSESSION - POSSESSION

PSYCHO-SPIRITUAL TERMS for the conditions, less than Possession, that respond to the commands of authority to dispel forces of Evil are called Oppression and Obsession.

In a state of **OPPRESSION**, people experience attacks of evil spirit from outside of themselves. The most common characteristic of oppression is a sense of heaviness about the head. Frequently people find it difficult to think out a situation or persevere in a task. They feel discouraged and impeded by alien pressures; that is, forces not coming from within themselves.

Such persons alone, or in prayer with another, should command in the name of Jesus that the spirit of oppression leave and not return.

In the case of **OBSESSION**, the evil spirits are in a position to create severe disturbances in a particular area within a person. There is an actual presence within the person, though. That presence is **NOT** in a position to control the person. The person can still exercise free will in determining his or her life. The person can also expel the evil spirits, though often, another person is necessary to assist or direct the deliverance.

The person ministering deliverance should have the obsessed person utilize as much spiritual authority as possible. In obsession, the goal is to have the person obsessed arrive at the point of repenting of all past sins and present sinful attitudes, renounce the spirit obsessing them and with the minister, command such spirit or spirits in the name of Jesus to depart and not return.

BOTH OPPRESSION AND OBSESSION may require a physical examination and psychiatric assessment to deal with personal issues for the deliverance and healing to take place. Specific diseases, like Parkinson's disease, can cause certain psychotic manifestations as well as chemical deficiencies. Both have medical therapy treatments. This is why before praying for deliverance, I ask the person if they have talked to a medical doctor or psychiatrist about their experience.

In other words, don't assume that evil spirits are attacking the person or entities no matter what they see or hear. If you do assume that and jump right in praying for deliverance, this may be counter-productive by falsely suggesting and confirming that the person is experiencing the demonic and may even be possessed. **NOT GOOD**!

POSSESSION: Put simply, when a person's Mind and Will have been totally overtaken by a demon/s, they are unable to choose to deliver themselves from the demonic possession and are in need of external help, an Exorcist.

WHEN AN EXORCISM IS NEEDED

Many times a person just needs spiritual or medical help, especially if drugs or other addictions are present. The specially trained priest and medical professionals will be able to work together to address the patient, and be able to determine what type of illness the patient is suffering from.

After the need of the person has been determined then the appropriate help will be met. In offering spiritual help, prayers may be offered, the laying on of hands or a counseling session may be prescribed. The exorcist may not perform an exorcism if he does not know the person.

SIGNS OF DEMONIC POSSESSION

Signs of demonic invasion vary depending on the type of demon and its purpose, including:

- **Speaking or understanding another language which they had never learned before**

- **Intense hatred and violent reaction toward all religious objects or items**

- **Antipathy towards entering a church, speaking Jesus' name or hearing scripture**

- **Knowledge of things that they should not have.**

- **Supernatural physical strength not subject to the person's build or age**

- Change in the person's voice

- Cutting, scratching, and biting of skin

- Unnatural bodily postures/ change in the person's face and body

- Losing control of their normal personality and entering into a frenzy or rage, and/or attacking others

- **Levitation, moving of objects**

CAUTION: With all this talk about Evil and Deliverance, don't start looking for Satan and Evil in everything and everybody. Evil loves your attention and curiosity. Do not give it one iota of your attention.

Keep your focus and attention on the Lord with you, and if you feel tempted or finding yourself thinking about it too much, simply tell it to "Get lost in the name of Jesus" and forget about it.

JESUS:
- "The power that is in **You** now is greater than the powers that are in the world."

- "While you are in the world you will suffer, but don't be afraid of it or let your hearts be troubled, because **I overcame my fear of it and so can you**, because I am with you."

FEAR:

Fear is the greatest power of Satan, demons, and evil, to control individuals, family members, governments and their leaders, religion and their leaders, and to what end?
The great plan of Satan from the beginning is to return to rule the universe, the one world government and humanity, **as the one god.**

*The goal of all his followers, Satanists, Luciferians, and those possessed, who choose his path to immortality and pleasure, is to bring it about. *(The end of time with Satan as the god of this world and the universe)*

HOW? CONTROLLING ANY OPPOSITION USING:

- FEAR OF SUFFERING AND DEATH
- FEAR OF EVIL *(So Evil and Satan can go unopposed)*
- FEAR OF THE UNKNOWN
- FEAR OF BEING CANCELLED IF YOU SPEAK THE TRUTH
- FEAR OF BEING CAST OUT, MARGINALIZED, AND ELIMINATED   *(So Evil can go unopposed)*

CHAPTER 8

DELIVERANCE RITUALS

FOR THOSE WHO WANT TO DENOUNCE SATAN AND EVIL, REPENT, BE SAVED, CHOOSE ETERNAL LIFE, AND REJECT IMMORTAL DEATH.

IMPORTANT: The following are Rituals for Deliverance, **NOT** Exorcism. When using any of these rituals, you need to apply an "attitude." Do **NOT** show any signs of **FEAR**, no matter what you see, hear or feel. It's OK to be startled, but immediately respond by focusing on Jesus with you, then get in there and attack. When you are done attacking, attack again, and punish them with the name and blood of Jesus until they leave. The more you do it, the easier it gets and they will be afraid of you, instead of you them.

DELIVERANCE RITUAL #1
(Simple deliverance)

"Jesus, in your name and the blood you shed on the Cross, I bind and cast out whoever and whatever Evil you are that is attacking me. I command you, to leave and go to Hell where you belong. Jesus is the Lord of my Life. Amen.

DELIVERANCE RITUAL #2
(For minor attacks of oppression and for obsession)

God, my creator and Lord, forgive me for allowing Satan, Demons, Powers and Spirits to temp and seduce me with Power, Sex, Money, and Pleasure. Forgive me for all the things I have let Evil obsess and addict me to. I am truly sorry for all the Sins of my entire life that have destroyed me and I have destroyed others.

Jesus, by the Unconditional Love you had for me on the cross, forgive my sins and give me the strength to change my life.

DELIVERANCE PRAYER:
(In a Commanding Voice, directed at Satan and all Evil)

In your name, Jesus and by the blood You shed on the cross for me, and the Power and authority of the Holy Spirit, bind Satan and all evil spirits and powers attacking me. Punish them and cast them out.

I bind and cast you out and command you to go before the throne of God, your creator, to do with you as He wills.

Lord, grant me the grace to keep my attention on You here with me, and not take back these temptations and lies by thinking about or dwelling on them.

I am a child of God. I belong to You Jesus and You alone. You are the Lord of my life. Into Your hands, I commend my spirit.

Response: "Deliver me, Jesus"

FROM:

Fear and Anger... R.
Pride and Self-Righteousness... R.
Greed and Selfishness... R.
Envy and Jealousy... R.
Lust and Desires of the Flesh... R.
Hatred and Judging... R.

Doubt and Despair... R.
Self-Hatred... R.

Any legal rights Satan, Demons, Powers, and Principalities, that have a legal hold on me and my family back seven generations... **"Deliver me, Jesus"**

COMMIT TO JESUS AS THE LORD OF YOUR LIFE

- I surrender my entire mind, body, and spirit to You, Jesus, my Lord and Savior and no other.

- I refuse to be mastered by Sin and Evil.

- I renounce you, Satan, and all of your lies and empty promises.

- I bind and cast you out by my love for Jesus.

OUR FATHER who art in Heaven, hallowed be Thy name.

Thy Kingdom come, Thy will be done, on Earth as it is in Heaven. Give me this day, my daily bread, and forgive me my sins as I forgive those who have sinned against me. And lead me out of temptation and **DELIVER ME FROM EVIL**. Amen.

Glory to You, my Creator and Father, and to my Lord and Friend, Jesus the Christ, and You the Holy Spirit, the Unconditional Love and Wisdom of God, as it was in the beginning, is now, and ever shall be. **AMEN, ALLELUIA!**

*(If you are attacked again, you attack and torture Evil, whoever and whatever they are with the above prayers until they leave. Then go and enjoy life, because the reason He gives us power over temptation and Evil is to have JOY, LIFE and PEACE, **so get to it!**)*

YOU ARE IN A BATTLE FOR YOUR LIFE AND ETERNAL SOUL.

YOU MAY LOSE BATTLES, BUT WITH JESUS YOU WIN THE WAR.

ALLELUIA JESUS!!!

DELIVERANCE RITUAL #3
(For those evil spirits and demons that require more prayer and fasting)

PRAYER OF CONFESSION AND FORGIVENESS

Response: Lord, forgive me.

LORD, IF I HAVE

- Spent less time with you and drifted away from my faith... **Lord, forgive me!**
- Judged, gossiped, and hurt others... R.

- Lusted, watched pornography and used others sexually... R.

- Held grudges and wanted to hurt someone... R.

- Been involved in any occult practices and rituals, or with people involved with these evil powers... R.

- Been selfish, greedy, and have not participated in service ministry for the poor, sick, and the marginalized... R.

- Allowed Evil to attach itself to my body, mind and spirit, because of the pleasure and the power it gave me... R.

- Abused alcohol, drugs, and prescription medications... R.

- Abused others and allowed myself to be abused... R.

PRAYER FOR POWER OF DELIVERANCE

Lord God, You who created me, and You our Lord and Friend, Jesus the Christ, grant me/us the power and authority to bind and cast out and trample on Satan, Demons, Powers and Evil Spirits **Amen.**

PRAYER OF DELIVERANCE

Response: In the name of Jesus, I cast you out.

- All powers, principalities, rulers from the kingdom of darkness... **In the name of Jesus, I cast you out.**

- The spirits in charge in this oppression, obsession, and seducing my Will... R.

- Spirits and demons of fear and lies... R.

- Spirits and demons of lust, sex abuse and rape... R.

- Spirits and demons of violence and hatred... R.

- Spirits and demons of physical abuse... R.

- All demons, spirits, powers of addiction and disease that have a hold on_____'s body, mind, feelings and will... R.
- All contacts and participation in occult practices,

rituals, curses, witchcraft, use of articles of darkness and evil... R.

(Hold a crucifix and sprinkle holy water in four directions. And in a commanding voice read the following)

I cast out every unclean spirit, every Satanic power, every attack of the powers of darkness, every legion and principality, in the name of my Lord Jesus Christ.

THE HOLY SPIRIT CRUSHES you Satan and all Evil Demons and Spirits with the knowledge and truth of your future and eternal damnation.

- **For all eternity** you will dwell in darkness with no experience or hope of light that you betrayed and lost.

- **For all eternity**, you have lost your former state.

- **For all eternity**, you will experience pain, but your bodies will not die.

- For all eternity, you will be imprisoned in hell without hope.

- **For all eternity** you will experience no love, no power, no pleasure, and no light, only darkness and despair.

- **For all eternity**, you will live in chaos and destroy one another without end.

- **For all eternity**, you are damned, cursed, despised, and powerless.

- **For all eternity**, you will be tortured, tormented, experience all the horrific suffering you caused humanity from the beginning.

- **For all eternity**, you will never see or experience God or the light of divinity.

- **You will lose** all the divine knowledge that you infected humanity with.

- **You will rot** in the very evil you created.

- All your gates, links, and pathways to your hierarchy of evil from the least of spirits to Satan will be no more.

- The Holy Spirit tortures, scourges, and causes you the greatest pain and suffering to all the Evil that has tempted, seduced and possessed me.

THE RESURRECTION and re-creation of Jesus' physical body, which he will grant to those who believe, and lead us through the portal to heaven, **CASTS YOU OUT**

- **The Resurrection** destroyed your powers of fear, sin, and death.

- **The Resurrection** raises us to the heights of Heaven as the God's children.

- **The Resurrection** will torment you now and forever with the knowledge that God has given to us what you never had and will never know or experience for all eternity.

- You who seduced and experimented with our physical bodies and minds and brought sin, suffering, and death into the world and us, have now been undone by Christ's Resurrection.

- **The Resurrection** casts you out with the knowledge of what you lost for lust and power, and condemned yourselves for all eternity. You are the most stupid and pathetic of all created beings.

- **The blood of Christ and His Resurrection** breaks and destroys all bonds, legal rights and holds on my mind, body and soul, back to 10 generations of my family.

- Your time here Satan is over. I will continue to torture you until you leave.

RENOUNCING SATAN, EVIL, AND CHOOSING JESUS TO BE THE LORD OF YOUR LIFE

Lord, grant me peace, Unconditional Love, and fill me with the Holy Spirit as I renounce Satan, all evil, and profess my faith and love for you, Father, Son, and Holy Spirit.

- **I renounce** you Satan and all your works and your empty promises.

- **I renounce sin**, so as to live in the freedom of the children of God.

- **I renounce the lure of evil** so that sin may have no mastery or legal rights over me.

- **I renounce Satan**, the Tempter and Seducer.

- I believe in God, the Father Almighty, Creator of Heaven and Earth Jesus Christ, His only Son, my Lord and friend, who was born of the Virgin Mary, suffered death, was buried, but rose from the dead, and is seated at the right hand of the Father.

- I do believe in the Holy Spirit, all my sisters and brothers in my church family, the communion of Saints, that our sins are forgiven, the resurrection of my body, and eternal life forever. **Amen.**

Lord, bless, watch over and protect me, my family, and all of us, in the name of the Father, Son, and Holy Spirit.

AMEN- ALLELUIA!

Those who have read this book and labeled it as just **Religious Crap, Fiction,** and **seek to Trash** and **Cancel** it, **BEWARE**!

You have been seduced by **Power** and **Self-righteousness** and have chosen to join the path of Satan and become his instrument of Evil.

CHAPTER 9

BE CAREFUL WHAT YOU CHOOSE,
You may end up getting it for all eternity.

- The only thing Satan and Evil can give you is Power, Sex, Money, and Pleasure while you are here in your physical bodies through your **physical Senses**.

- When your physical body dies and your Consciousness, Mind, and Will are separated from it, how the heck are you going to experience the Physical sensual pleasures of Sex, Power, Money, and Hedonism?

- Your Physical Earthly body and senses will be dead and 'cold lunch' for worms and maggots.

- Even if you don't believe in any of this or that there is no afterlife, this is a terrifying and horrific destiny that you cannot escape.

- This is the World and Universe that Satan and Evil destroyed and their eternal dwelling place and Hell that they created.

- What if their motivation for seducing you and me by physical desires and pleasure is to, distract, addict, and keep us from heaven, eternal Life, and God's Unconditional Love that Satan and the fallen angels lost.

Everything then, that Satan offers, is only temporary and will end with no hope for it to continue after your physical death.

- What if Satan's only pleasure is not physical, because he and the minions of Demons bodies died?

- What if their only pleasure is tempting, seducing, and enslaving us to worship them so they can be gods; experiencing pleasure by destroying and watching us destroy each other and creation.

- What if Satan and Evil's only way to retaliate against God is to destroy us, because God destroyed their offspring *(The offspring from fallen angels with human women)*

- What if they hate us because God has forgiven us and not them for what they did and continue to do to us and his creation?

- What if they want us to share in their eternal suffering and misery when our bodies die, with no more physical senses to experience Sex, Pleasure, and Power.

- What if they SEDUCED, ADDICTED, LIED, and you have and are choosing their temporary pleasures?

What if it is a LIE? If it is, you have been and are SCREWED.

As Jesus said, "**Satan is a Deceiver and Liar from the beginning.**"

CHOOSE UNCONDITIONAL LOVE AND ETERNAL LIFE!

YOUR FUTURE IF YOU DO NOT!

HELL: Nothingness, No God, No Love, No Light, No Peace, No Pleasure or Power, only Suffering, Torment, Isolation, Loneliness, No Hope, No Escape, and No Coffee Breaks!

PROOF OF HEAVEN

NEUROSURGEON Dr. Eben Alexander:

"I have spent decades, as a neurosurgeon and scientist, at some of the most prestigious medical institutions, but because of my coma and NEAR DEATH experience, I know beyond a doubt that our consciousness lives on after our physical brains and bodies die. We are actually set free to a higher level of knowing, and that the universe is defined by an Unconditional Love for us. And that Unconditional Love is God." (<u>Proof of Heaven</u>, by Dr. Eben Alexander)

Dr. Eben Alexander is a Harvard-trained Brain Surgeon who was an agnostic, but not anymore. He had a near-death experience of God and Heaven. For more of his incredible story, his book is entitled Proof of Heaven. You can also find a wonderful convincing interview on YouTube. I highly recommend reading his story as he details his experience, not just of God and Heaven, but something that happened to him there that convinced him, without a doubt, that this all took place outside of his brain and physical body.

I included this story, because I not only believe it is true, but it represents a credible person, a Harvard trained Brain Surgeon, in his video interview on You tube, shows you the brain scans that reveal that the cortex was totally infected and non-functioning.

HEAVEN IS REAL and so isn't HELL

HEAVEN: ACCORDING TO THE NEW TESTAMENT

#1
"Brothers and sisters:
Behold, I tell you a mystery. We shall not all fall asleep, but we will all be changed in an instant, in the blink of an eye, at the last trumpet, for the trumpet will sound, the dead will be raised incorruptible and we shall all be changed. For that which is corruptible must clothe itself with incorruptibility and that which is mortal must clothe itself with immortality. Then the word that is written shall come about:

> 'Death is swallowed up in victory. Where, O Death, is your victory? Where, O Death, is your sting?'

Thanks be to God who gives us the victory through our Lord Jesus Christ." (1 Cor. 15: 51-57)

#2
"We do not want you to be unaware, brothers and sisters, about those who have fallen asleep, so that you may not grieve like the rest, who have no hope.

For if we believe that Jesus died and rose, so too will God, through Jesus, bring with him those who have fallen asleep.

Indeed, we tell you this, on the word of the Lord, that we who are alive, who are left until the coming of the Lord, will surely not precede those who have fallen asleep." (I Thess. 4:13-18)

#3
"Brothers and sisters,
our citizenship is in heaven and from it we also await our savior, the Lord Jesus Christ. He will change our lowly body to conform with his glorified Body by the power that enables him also to bring all things into subjection to himself." (Phil. 3:20-21)

#4
"Brothers and Sisters,
We know that if our earthly body, a tent should be destroyed, we have a building from God, a dwelling not made with hands, eternal in heaven. And so, we are always courageous, although we know that while we are in these earthly bodies we are away from the Lord, for we walk and live by Faith, not by what we see."
(2 Cor. 5: 6-10)

#5
"Therefore, we are not discouraged rather, although our outer self is wasting away, our inner self is being strengthened and renewed day by day. For this momentary suffering that will pass away is producing for us an eternal glory that is beyond all comparison." (2 Cor. 4:16-18)

"Come, follow me, and enter the Kingdom that I have prepared for you from the beginning of time."

APPENDIX

I condemned no individual or group in this book. That is reserved for the God who created us and Him alone.

I also intentionally excluded naming specific persons locally, nationally, or internationally, as well as those in the middle of major issues in the United States or any other country.

The reason is that the God I have come to believe in and know, unconditionally loves all of humankind and that includes especially those who don't believe and curse Him.

While we are still in these earthly physical bodies, the greatest gift God has given us is our FREE WILL. Why, because with it we can choose to LOVE, which we were created to give and receive.

Because of Satan and Evil, there is a darkness in us that wants to seduce, addict, and destroy our Spirit and Soul. Every day we are faced with choices between Good and Evil.

It is these choices that all of us, that includes you and me, that will determine our future life in Heaven with the God who created us, or Hell with Satan.

As Jesus said, **He condemns no one**. By our choices and actions, we condemn ourselves.

GOD AND HIS COMMANDMENTS ARE
WHAT MATTERS

"The commandment I leave you is this, I want you to Love one another, not as you love, but the way I have loved you."

"Love consists of this, not that we believe and love God, rather that He has loved us first."

BIBLIOGRAPHY

- **KEEP THEM BUSY,** article by Ralph Andrus

- **SCRIPTURE,** NIB, New International Bible

- **COPIED SECTIONS** from book, **"ATTACKING EVIL THAT IS ATTACKING YOU",** by Fr. Francis Pompei ofm

- **ABORTION PHOTOS,** *Center for Bio-Ethical Reform as the copyright holder by printing "Copyright abortionNO.org"*

- **JESUS CRUCIFIED ETCHING,** Jillian Fabrizi, artist, Syracuse, New York

- **FACE OF JESUS,** Mary Jo Woyciesjes, artist, Syracuse, New York

- **OPPRESSION, OBSESSION, POSSESSION ARTICLE, Prayers and Blessings from The Roman Ritual with Commentary,** Michael Scanlon, T.O.R, The College of Steubenville, Steubenville, Ohio, 43952

- **PHOTOS:**
    1. **POINTING FINGER,** Free Clip Art

    2. **WOMAN IN HELL**- Trish Pompei, my Sister, the Editor, hoping it's not True- Ha Ha

    3. **MAN IN HELL**- Francis Pompei ofm, the Author, hoping also it's not True-

"For all those struggling with Satan and Evil tempting you with Power, Money, Sex, Hedonism, Anger, Hatred, and Violence for any issue or reason, this book, God, and I are **NOT your enemy**,

I am"

Fr. Francis C. Pompei ofm
(Author)

www.ingramcontent.com/pod-product-compliance
Lightning Source LLC
Chambersburg PA
CBHW071117030426
42336CB00013BA/2120